Social Media Strategies for Kickstarter Campaigns

Table of Contents

Campaigns are like a race, a lot depend on good starts. Social media offers the platform for a good start.

— Narendra Modi

Chapter 1. Introduction

Are you ready to unbox the key to a successful Kickstarter campaign? In the digital age, nothing propels a campaign to stardom like a bullet-proof social media strategy. Welcome to our Special Report on Social Media Strategies for Kickstarter Campaigns - a comprehensive exploration, aimed to elevate your campaign to elseworldly heights. Whether you're launching a tech gadget or a children's book, this report is your map to the treasure of campaign success. Our strategies are easy to understand, highly effective, and tailored for all projects and scopes. Get ready to skyrocket those pledges and send your ideas into the orbit of reality! Now is the time to motivate, engage, and boost your Kickstarter campaign into the social media stratosphere. So what are you waiting for? Let this Special Report be your rocket fuel to success!

Chapter 2. Understanding Kickstarter: Envisaging Your Campaign Journey

In the enchanting universe of crowd-funding, Kickstarter reigns king. The platform continues to be a launching pad for ideas ranging from quaint children's books to revolutionary tech innovations. Before delving into the wellspring of Kickstarter strategies, it becomes paramount to comprehend the fundamental mechanics, philosophy, and dynamics of the platform itself. This understanding fosters a comprehensive vision of your campaign journey, paving the way to your project's promising future.

2.1. A Brief Introduction

Kickstarter is an eternity pool of creativity, offering innovators across the globe a platform to raise funds for their projects from generous and supportive backers. The platform operates on an 'all-or-nothing' model, which means that you either reach your set monetary goal within a stipulated time frame, or all the pledges are returned to the backers. Success on Kickstarter doesn't delineate merely reaching the fundraising goal, but surpassing it to a significant extent.

2.2. Understanding the Kickstarter Philosophy

Kickstarter is not a business start-up platform, nor is it an e-commerce website. It is essentially a public platform that bridges creators and communities together. Creators share their ideas, and if communities resonate with those, they pledge their support in terms of funding. This networking dynamo enables creators and innovators to test their ideas, assess public reactions, and gain validation for their projects before launching them on a grand scale. Kickstarter embodies the ethos of democratic creativity, empowering innovators worldwide to bring their ideas to life while also involving their backers in the creative process.

2.3. Kickstarter's Campaign Structure

Each Kickstarter campaign is divided into key segments – project idea, funding goals, rewards, and timeline. Your project idea includes a detailed description of your project and what you plan to accomplish with it. Funding goals represent the sum you need to bring your project to life. Rewards are the elements you offer to the backers in return for their pledges, differentiating them by pledge amounts. The timeline represents the duration your campaign will be live on Kickstarter, generally ranging from 1 to 60 days.

2.4. Building Your Campaign

Having a comprehensive vision of your campaign journey necessitates a thorough roadmap that charts every detail of your project. Begin by defining your project, its goals, feasibility, uniqueness, and value proposition. Subsequently, establish stringent, transparent, and realistic funding goals that account for manufacturing, shipping, and unforeseen expenses.

Rewards should be meticulously crafted to ensure they are aligned with the pledge amounts. Remember, backers are not investors looking for a profit, but enthusiasts who believe in and want to be a part of your project. Tailor your rewards to acknowledge their support, making them feel integral to your endeavor.

Determining the campaign timeline would depend on the complexity of your project, the budget requirement, and your marketing strategies. Shorter campaigns usually draw more attention, as they induce a sense of urgency and excitement. But consider the trade-off carefully - shorter campaigns leave less space for error and recovering momentum, once lost, could be challenging.

2.5. Cultivating a Community

Kickstarter is a distinctive blend of crowd-funding and community-building. Your backers are more than mere donors; they form a community of supporters who share your vision. Treating your backers as integral members of your project's journey and involving them in the creative process fosters a more engaged community. Regular updates, surveys, and sneak peeks promote interaction and inclusiveness. Many successful Kickstarter projects have witnessed their backers transforming into brand ambassadors, highlighting the impact of a nurtured community on your campaign's success.

Kickstarter encapsulates a dynamic ecosystem revolving around creativity, innovation, and community engagement. Understanding its milieu thoroughly assists in devising tactical strategies, setting realistic goals, and ultimately steering your campaign towards success. Once this foundation has been laid, the journey to the stars becomes much smoother, promising, and exhilarating. Armed with a clear vision of your campaign's trajectory, the fields of social media strategies that follow will be a fertile ground to sow seeds of success. From selecting platforms to creating compelling content, leveraging video power to engaging effectively, our next chapters will elucidate them all. So buckle up, and let's emblazon the Kickstarter sky with the shooting star of your campaign!

Chapter 3. Winning with Social Media: An Overview

In the digital age, social media has seeped into every nook and cranny of our lives. Kickstarter campaigns are no exception. This omnipresent platform offers a plethora of opportunities to campaign owners looking to attract, engage, and convert potential backers. This chapter acts as your compass, steering you through the landscape of social media, unlocking its full potential to achieve your campaign goals.

3.1. Social Media: A Key in the Kickstarter Ecosystem

Platforms like Facebook, Twitter, Instagram, YouTube, and LinkedIn have made it possible to reach the global audience without the boundaries of physical constraints. They have evolved from mere communication channels into powerful marketing tools, creating an ecosystem that nurtures crowd-funded projects. Social media platforms allow for a diverse range of content to be showcased - text, images, videos, live interactions, and more. These content types cater to a wide gamut of audience preferences, helping campaigns make a wider impact.

The first step towards winning with social media is to understand the role they play in your Kickstarter journey. They provide the stage for your pre-launch buzz, fuel your campaign during its run-time, and help maintain the momentum post-campaign. Social media platforms also serve as a two-way communication bridge between you, the campaign owner, and the backers, making it an invaluable tool for community building.

3.2. Understanding and Leveraging Social Media Algorithms

To truly tap into the power of social media and use it to propel your Kickstarter campaign forward, you need to understand and leverage the algorithms that govern these platforms. Every social media platform uses complex algorithms that determine what content gets visibility and what doesn't. Understanding these algorithms is like cracking a code - it gives you the potential to maximize your campaign reach, engagement, and eventually, success.

Algorithms analyze a variety of factors from a user's behavior - what they like, what they share, who they follow, how much time they spend on a post, and much more. By aligning your campaign with these preferences, you can ensure your campaign fits into the visibility criteria of the algorithm, thereby reaching more potential backers.

3.3. Choosing Your Primary Social Media Platforms

Not all social media platforms are equal, and no campaign can successfully manage to have a strong presence on all platforms simultaneously. Hence, it's crucial to identify the platforms where your potential backers are most active and focus your energies there.

User demographics like age, gender, geography, interests, and behavior patterns play a vital role in identifying which platforms will work best for your campaign. For instance, a tech gadget might find more success on a platform like Facebook or Reddit, known for their tech-savvy user base. In contrast, a fashion accessory might trend on Instagram due to its visual appeal and the platform's user preference.

3.4. Building Your Social Media Strategy

Now that you have an understanding of the role of social media, its algorithm, and have identified your primary platforms, you can start sculpturing your strategy. This includes deciding your campaign's tone of voice, creating a content calendar, integrating SEO best practices in content creation, and setting up a schedule for consistent posting.

Crafting the right strategy can effectively increase engagements and pull more backers your way. A successful strategy is well-thought-out, meticulously planned, and responsive to the audience's feedback, needs, and behavior patterns.

In the following chapters, we will go deeper into each of these aspects, sharpening your understanding and helping you build a robust social media strategy. You will learn how to craft compelling content, harness the power of video, and navigate through other crucial areas like paid advertising, influencer marketing, and post-campaign strategies.

By the end of this journey, you will no longer see social media as just a marketing tool. Instead, it will be your ally, your reliable navigator guiding you to the treasure trove of Kickstarter success.

Chapter 4. Choosing the Right Platforms for Your Campaign

Social media platforms come in myriad shapes and sizes, each with its specific features, advantages, and user demographics. Therefore, choosing the appropriate platforms is a critical first step for launching a successful Kickstarter campaign. Your choice should be driven by an analysis of your target audience map, the type of your campaign or product, and the unique qualities of each of these platforms.

4.1. Defining Your Target Audience

In an ideal world, your campaign would reach all corners of the globe in seconds. However, the reality is significantly more complex. You need to intimately know your target audience: their interests, social habits, online haunts, and behaviors. It's only through this understanding that you're able to be strategic in choosing the right social media platform for your Kickstarter campaign.

Start by brainstorming an audience persona. This hypothetical representation of your ideal backer would include demographics like age, gender, location, and occupation, along with psychographic characteristics such as attitudes, hobbies, and lifestyle. For example, if you are launching a tech gadget, your key audience might be young professionals (age 25-40), tech-savvy, with a preference for innovative, problem-solving gadgets.

Once you've defined your audience persona, cross-reference this with social media demographic breakdowns. For example, it's reported that younger users flock towards platforms such as Instagram and Snapchat, while an older audience pervades Facebook and LinkedIn. Quartz, Pew Research Centre, and a vast array of statistics hubs provide up-to-date analysis and infographics to help with this task.

4.2. Assessing Social Media Platform Characteristics

Each platform comes with distinctive qualities. Therefore, having a fair understanding of these will help zero in on the platforms which complement your campaign the best. Be aware, different platforms serve different types of content best. And that content's appeal can significantly differ across platforms.

Twitter strives on quick exchanges, trending topics, and hashtag conversations. It's particularly effective for real-time engagement and updates on your Kickstarter project. In contrast, Instagram is a visual platform that thrives on high-quality images and videos. If your product can be presented visually and looks appealing, this could be your go-to platform. On the other hand, Facebook bridges these two worlds and offers a wide range of features, from photo sharing, video hosting, event organization, and much more. However, the platform has shifted more toward pay-to-play, so be prepared to allocate a budget for ads. Lastly, LinkedIn is typically more business-oriented and could be best for B2B (Business to Business) campaigns.

4.3. Matching Product Type to Social Platforms

Being aware of your product type and how it resonates with the intended audience on a social platform can be a significant determinant of your campaign's success. A rule of thumb would be to match your product type with the kind of content that performs well on a platform.

For instance, visual products, such as design-oriented tech gadgets, handmade crafts, or fashion accessories, thrive on Instagram. If you're producing a comic book or graphic novel, platforms like Pinterest, with robust comic-loving communities, might work well. For tech products catered to businesses, marketing on LinkedIn could be beneficial. If your Kickstarter project is focused on community building or some form of social cause, Facebook, with its numerous community-centric features, would work in your favor.

4.4. Strategizing for Multiple Social Media Platforms

Don't box yourself into using just one platform. Using multiple platforms lets you appeal to a wider audience and provide different types of content. A diversified, yet focused, social media strategy is often the most effective.

However, remember that each platform requires a unique approach; 'Copy-Pasting' the same messages across platforms is not ideal. What works for Instagram doesn't necessarily work for Twitter or LinkedIn. Always alter your content to fit the tone and format of the platform in question.

4.5. Taking Advantage of Alternative and Niche Platforms

Mainstream platforms like Facebook, Instagram, and Twitter may hog the limelight, but don't overlook alternative platforms. Niche platforms like Reddit or Tumblr have engaged communities that might be relevant to your campaign. Websites like Product Hunt or Hacker News could be beneficial for tech campaigns. Similarly, Behance and Dribbble cater to a community of designers and creatives who may be interested in backing a project like theirs.

To conclude, choosing the right social media platforms is all about knowing your audience, understanding the strengths of each platform, and figuring out how your product fits into this equation. With these points in mind, your Kickstarter campaign is well on its way to becoming a captivator of attention and an engager of audiences around the digital landscape.

Chapter 5. Crafting Compelling Social Media Content

This stage is the bedrock of your social media strategy - crafting compelling social media content. It's the linchpin that holds all the other elements of your campaign together. It not only spreads the word about your project but also intriguingly communicates your vision that resonates with your target audience. So let's delve deeper into the world of appealing social media content that amplifies your campaign's potential.

5.1. Understanding Your Target Audience

Before we step into the world of content creation, it's crucial to understand your target audience. Your communication's success hinges on how well your content resonates with those who view it. Hence, start by defining your audience's demographic and psychographic profiles. Are they tech enthusiasts hunting for the next innovative gadget or parents interested in nurturing their children's reading habits? Understanding their tastes, preferences, pain points, and what appeals to them can guide you in crafting content that strikes a chord. Analyze your audience's behavior on social media - what they share, comment on, and the conversations they participate in. Such details can provide you fruitful insights to frame your content that sparks their interest.

5.2. Diverse Content Formats

Content does not have to be strictly textual. Social media opens the doors to a variety of content formats. Long and short-form videos, photos, infographics, live streams, polls, quizzes, and call-to-action posts can all play a part in drawing your audience towards your campaign.

Videos, in particular, have increased in popularity as they are capable of disseminating your idea effectively. A well-made explainer video demonstrating your product's use-case scenarios can work wonders.

Images and infographics can unravel the complex aspects of your product in a visually appealing and easy-to-understand format. Don't underestimate the power of succinctly powerful infographics - they're shareable, and they tend to stay with the user.

However, don't stick to a single content format. Mix it up to maintain the element of surprise and keep your content fresh. Experimenting with different formats will help you understand what your audience responds to the best.

5.3. Craft a Compelling Narrative

Storytelling has a unique charm. It's an art that taps into the emotions of your audience, transcending the usual buy-sell dynamic. Your Kickstarter campaign isn't merely a sales pitch; it's a story of your vision, aspiration, and journey. Don't merely present your product; narrate your journey. Speak about your struggles, your eureka moments. Your audience loves to know the 'why' behind your product. So, create a narrative that encapsulates your endeavor.

5.4. User-Generated Content

User-generated content (UGC) like testimonials, reviews, and user-experiences play a pivotal role in creating credibility for your campaign. People tend to trust the word of others who have experienced your product. UGC can prove to be a powerful weapon, allowing you to show authentic feedback and positive experiences related to your campaign. Encourage backers and early adopters to share their thoughts and experiences. Spotlight your backers and make them feel celebrated; they are, after all, the supporters of your dream.

5.5. Consistency is Key

Maintain a consistent voice across social media platforms. Consistency in your message and tone assists in creating a brand image that sticks. A seamless experience across platforms helps your audience recognize and remember your campaign. Don't confuse them by continually changing the tone, style, or values you communicate. Maintain synchronization between all your social media efforts.

Ultimately, creating compelling social media content is an ongoing process. It's about understanding your audience, experimenting with different content formats, narrating a compelling story, leveraging user-generated content, and maintaining consistency in your message. With this potent mix, your social media content won't just inform your audience about your campaign; it will invite them in, make them feel part of your journey, evoke an emotional response, and encourage them to contribute towards making your dream a reality. So, gear up, and let your creativity lead your campaign to a successful launch and beyond.

Chapter 6. Unleashing the Power of Video Content on Social Media

The advent of the digital age unlocks new vistas of brand promotion and engagement. One primary tool is video content, and it's a beast we're about to tame. Wildly popular, overwhelmingly impactful, and inexplicably potent in reaching to the crannies of your potential backers' psyche, video content presents your Kickstarter campaign with unsurpassed opportunities to communicate your narrative, stir emotions, and push engagement like never before.

6.1. Harnessing the Emotional Power of Video

Emotion is an enormous driving factor behind most decisions people make, including a decision to back a Kickstarter project. Thus, creating a video could provide the perfect medium to convey feelings of passion, positivity, or urgency about your project. Given its visual and auditory combination, it can foster a stronger connection and empathy between your campaign and potential backers, allowing you to outshine other campaigns that only rely on static images and text.

Be conscious about the positioning of your video, the emotions it emits, and the narrative it tells. A well-crafted video might present a touching personal story, a sneak peek into how the product is manufactured, or simply a joyous celebration of your dreams turning into reality. Never forget - every second is crucial, and each moment must be meticulously designed to propel the viewer's emotions.

6.2. High-Quality Production: Not an Option, but a Requirement

Living in an era of ceaseless digital innovations has raised the public's expectations concerning the quality of video content. A poorly produced video can easily tarnish the credibility of your Kickstarter campaign, causing potential supporters to question the quality of your project. Thus, high-quality production is no longer an option, but a fundamental necessity.

It doesn't inherently mean investing enormous amounts into professional studios and high-end gear - a basic understanding of lighting, sound, and image stability can make a significant difference. Regardless of your budget, you must aim to deliver crisp images, clear audio, and overall polished visuals to optimize viewer experience.

6.3. The Power of 'How it Works' Videos

Backers love to be a part of innovative, game-changing ideas. Understanding the nuts and bolts of your project can spark their curiosity and increase their confidence in your project, making them more willing to offer their support. Crafting a 'How it Works' video can be an effective strategy to demonstrate the functionality, features, and benefits of your offering.

For tech gadgets, it could be about a walkthrough of the gadget interface or software. For creative projects like a book or artwork, it's about showing the artistic process. Essentially, the aim is to demonstrate how your project stands out from the competition and why it's worth pledging.

6.4. Timing: Quick and Engaging

In the fast-paced digital landscape, attention is a scarce resource. It's crucial to ensure that your Kickstarter videos are quick, engaging, and to-the-point. A study from Wistia suggested that the optimum video length for viewer engagement is 2 minutes. Beyond this threshold, viewer engagement tends to decrease significantly. A well-made, engaging short video can leave a lasting impression and keep potential backers hooked.

However, this isn't a cookie-cutter approach. Depending on the complexity of a project, a longer video might be necessary. But even then, crucial points should be covered within the initial phase of the video to quickly capture the viewer's attention.

6.5. Call to Action: Igniting the Spark

What's a powerful Kickstarter video without a compelling call to action (CTA)? Always remember, the primary focus of your video isn't just about creating awareness for your project, it should also generate action from potential backers. Invite viewers to back your project, share your campaign, follow your social media channels, or sign up for your newsletter - the point is to drive positive action.

A well-crafted video content strategy can help your Kickstarter campaign gain substantial traction in the virtual world. It forms a visual bridge between your dreams and the potential supporters, establishing an emotional connection and leaving a mark on viewer's souls. Now that you've dived deep into the ocean of video content strategy, it's time to grab your gear and create your masterpiece that shapes your Kickstarter success story.

Chapter 7. Engaging with Your Audience: Successful Communication Tactics

The art of successful communication with your audience forms the bedrock of any successful Kickstarter campaign. This chapter deciphers the mysteries of effective audience engagement and reveals the secret sauces that can set your campaign alight in the digital sphere.

7.1. Establishing A Regular Pattern of Communication

Creating an anticipated pattern of consistent communication sets the platform for meaningful engagement with your audience. Regular updates can help to maintain the momentum of your campaign and keep your audience interested. With consistent, meaningful updates, you establish a reliable rhythm that signals to your backers that you're dedicated to your vision. Your followers are more than just observers, they are part of your journey. Therefore, timely and regular updates can enhance your project's transparency and trustworthiness. Be sure to share stories, insights, and sneak peeks into your creative processes, making your community feel included and valued.

7.2. Creating Engaging Content

Good content is the nucleus of audience engagement. To make your content 'engaging,' you need to ensure it connects emotively with your audience and compels them to interact. Sharing real and authentic stories about your journey, the challenges you faced, and how you overcame those challenges, can inspire your audience and compel them to join your cause. These tales of struggle and triumph can be especially effective for Kickstarter campaigns as they tap into the audience's empathy and desire to support those who strive for their dreams. Furthermore, your content should be enriching and give your audience value, either by educating, entertaining, or inspiring them.

7.3. Encouraging Feedback and Participation

Inviting your audience to voice their thoughts and opinions not only fosters community, but also provides valuable insights into their needs and preferences. Hence, encourage backers to leave comments, ask questions, and express their opinions. Welcome feedback from your community, as it can lead to productive conversations and ideas that might even improve your campaign. Always respond to your backers in a manner that demonstrates you value their input and are dedicated to making improvements.

7.4. Using the Right Tone and Language

The way you communicate, the tone you use, and the language you choose can significantly impact how your message is received by your audience. It's crucial to use an approachable and relatable tone that makes your audience feel comfortable and understood. Be professional but avoid jargons that could alienate your followers. Develop a sharp sense of your audience's demographics and preferences to tailor your language and tone accordingly. Remember, using the appropriate language builds rapport, trust, and engagement with your audience.

7.5. Leveraging Visual Communication

Visuals form a substantial part of communication on social media platforms. The use of graphics, images, infographics, and videos can be a dynamic way to present information and draw attention. Highlight your project's unique aspects, display progress, emphasize urgency during the final campaign days, or initiate mini-campaigns within the main campaign through visually appealing content. Remember, a well-timed, captivating image or video can communicate more than words can in a mere glance.

7.6. Being Responsive and Proactive

In the world of social media, things move rapidly. Within this fast-paced environment, being responsive becomes pivotal. Quick responses to queries, concerns, or simply acknowledging the backers can provide a sense of care and dedication towards your project. Proactivity is just as important – anticipate your audience's needs, address their potential doubts even before they voice them, and regularly inform of your project's progress.

Finally, it's important to remember that engaging your audience is not a one-size-fits-all task. What creates a buzz for one campaign might not work for another. Therefore, always be open to experimentation, refinement, and most importantly, learning from your community. Understanding this chapter's tactics and implementing them will help you foster solid relationships with your audience, and such relationships often translate into a successful Kickstarter campaign. Your audience engagement strategy is, after all, a marathon, not a sprint. Be patient, persistent and always stay true to your vision.

Chapter 8. Boosting Campaign Visibility: Effective Use of Hashtags and SEO

The audacious challenge that confronts every Kickstarter campaign is penetrating through the dense fog of internet content and shining brightly to capture audience attention. An indispensable tool in your arsenal for achieving this feat is the meticulous application of Search Engine Optimization (SEO) and thoughtful hashtag use. These tools, when properly leveraged, have the power to amplify your campaign's visibility exponentially and invite a cascade of pledges that can propel your project to the zenith of success.

8.1. The Power and Purpose of Hashtags

The ongoing conversation in the vast world of social media has a cyclopean din that is often challenging to navigate without the guidance of markers. This is where hashtags come into play. These simple yet potent tools serve as categoric signposts guiding users to topics of their interest. They are like breadcrumbs that can lead potential backers to the enticing forest trail that is your campaign.

Hashtags are more than just a passing trend; they are a crucial tool to help your prospective backers locate your campaign. When used correctly, hashtags can go beyond commandeering traffic to your page. They can aid in establishing your brand, distinguishing your identity, and creating a community around your campaign. But use them irresponsibly, and they might obscure your message. A conscious strategy is essential for hashtag utilization.

Consider, for instance, your campaign is about launching an

innovative board game. A combination of popular and specific hashtags can work wonders. Some suggestions would be \#boardgames, \#tabletopgames, \#kickstartercampaign, and \#innovation. These tags cast a wide net across diverse interest pools while maintaining relevance.

Always accompany popular and generic tags with campaign-specific tags like \#YourBoardgameName. This hashtag, while not initially having significant reach, will help create a unique identity and community around your campaign over time. When you and your campaign followers use it, it quickly becomes a virtual home, a meeting place of enthusiasts rallied by your innovative project.

8.2. Understanding Search Engine Optimization (SEO)

As with the wider world of the internet, the vast expanse of Kickstarter projects poses a conundrum - how to be 'found.' Search Engine Optimization (SEO) is your golden key to unlock visibility. Search engines are the gateway through which most users access content online. Appearing in the top results is akin to having a prime high-street location for a retail store—visitor traffic and visibility are at a maximum.

SEO is the science and art of tweaking your campaign content and keywords to ensure it appears prominently in relevant search engine results. These results are determined by 'crawlers,' software that scour the internet, interpret and index content based on a set of parameters defined by the search engine. These typically include relevance, quality, and trustworthiness of content, which SEO strategies aim to enhance for higher ranking on the Search Engine Result Pages (SERPs).

Let's imagine your campaign is about publishing a graphic novel. Keywords that should appear frequently (but not excessively, as 'keyword stuffing' can be penalized) in your campaign description might include terms like "graphic novel," "comics," "illustration," "Kickstarter," and maybe the genre of your novel like "horror," "fantasy," or "romance." As per Kickstarter's browsing functionality, your campaign title is like the 'meta title' of a webpage, making it incredibly vital to incorporate pertinent keywords therein.

8.3. Implementing SEO and Hashtags Together

To truly maximize your campaign visibility, hashtags and SEO should work in harmony. The selection of hashtags should be guided by SEO principles. Find what's trending and relevant in your domain, weave those keywords into your campaign description, and generate hashtags from this word pool.

But, since social media platforms have their own search algorithms differing from typical search engines, be mindful that not all SEO-friendly terms make compelling hashtags and vice versa. Hence, adopting a balanced approach to applying both ensures you can leverage the best of these tools.

Collaterally, maintaining consistency in chosen keywords and hashtags across different platforms strengthens your campaign's identity. This coherence presents a unified front across search engines and social media platforms, increasing the chances of appearing in the audience's searches.

Conclusively, it is crucial to keep in mind that while careful handling of hashtags and SEO can help bolster your campaign's visibility, they're only a part of your campaign's holistic digital strategy. Be sure to harmonize these tools with the other strategies outlined in this comprehensive guide to see your Kickstarter Campaign rocket to success. Engage your audience effectively, continually optimize your strategy, stay adaptable, and watch as your dream project unfurls into reality.

Chapter 9. Unlocking the Potential of Paid Advertising on Social Media

Paid advertising on social media platforms is a powerful tool that can be employed to enhance the visibility and engagement levels of your Kickstarter campaign. It leverages the capability to target specific demographics and behaviors, provides detailed analytics to comprehend your audience better, and, most beneficially, is cost-efficient and can be adapted to fit any budget size.

9.1. Why is Paid Advertising Essential?

In a world populated by massive amounts of digital content, securing a meaningful visibility for your Kickstarter campaign is more challenging than ever before. Organic reach is viable, yet its effectiveness is often limited by algorithms that prioritize paid content. This is where paid advertising shows its strength.

Primarily, paid advertising can push your campaign in front of a larger and global audience, vastly expanding your reach beyond personal networks and regular followers. It amplifies the possibility of gaining attention, and subsequently pledges, from individuals who may not have stumbled upon your campaign otherwise.

Furthermore, social media platforms offer fine-tuned targeting options. This functionality allows you to identify and focus on individuals who are likely to be genuinely interested in your Kickstarter project, based on their hobbies, interests, and engagement history. This degree of precision is unrivalled by traditional marketing methods and can significantly boost your campaign's conversion rates.

Finally, paid advertising on social media provides in-depth analytics. You can study your ads' performance, gleaning valuable insights about your audience's preferences, behaviors, and engagement levels. This understanding can guide you to optimize your campaign and maximize your return on investment.

9.2. How to Choose the Right Platform for Paid Advertising

Determining the best platform for your paid advertising strategy often boils down to understanding where your target audience resides and how they interact with content.

Facebook and Instagram, with their massive user base and diverse demographics, are a prime choice for numerous Kickstarter campaigns. They offer an extensive suite of ad targeting options and content formats, ranging from static images, carousel ads, to immersive video experiences, and more.

Twitter leverages its fleet-of-foot nature with promoted tweets and trends, enabling your campaign to tap into real-time discussions and events quickly and intensely.

LinkedIn is ideal for campaigns targeting professionals or B2B markets, offering sponsored content and InMail to reach out to your audience directly.

YouTube ads, particularly for gadget or tech projects, can capitalize on the platform's visual nature, turning demonstration videos engaging and compelling.

9.3. Crafting Your Paid Advertisement Content

The content of your paid advertisement heavily influences its succeeding performance. It should be engagingly crafted, clearly articulating the essence and the value of your Kickstarter campaign.

Start with a compelling headline. This is the first point of contact with your audiences, and hence it should be catchy, crisp, and encapsulating the main proposition of your campaign.

The main body of the ad should further elucidate your project. Highlight its unique selling points, the problems it aims to solve, and the benefits it offers. Humanize your campaign by sharing the story behind your project, expressing authenticity and building an emotional connection with the audience.

Visual elements within the advertisement need to be striking and relevant. They should support the message, draw attention, and illustrate the project effectively. Depending on the platform, this might be a static image, a carousel or a video.

Lastly, always include a clear call-to-action. Intrigue your audience and prompt them to learn more about your project or make a pledge.

9.4. Understanding Paid Advertising Metrics

A proper understanding of metrics involved in paid advertising would facilitate better decision making, helping to refine and optimize your strategy according to audience response.

Clicks are the most immediate metric to gauge the interest your ad is generating. But to understand the real impact, we need to delve deeper. Metrics like 'Click-Through-Rate (CTR)', indicating the percentage of viewers who clicked your ad, 'Cost-per-Click (CPC)', giving an average cost for each click, 'Conversion Rate', measuring how many interactions resulted in a pledge, or 'Return on Ad Spend (ROAS)', evaluating the profitability of your ad spend, are vital.

Most social platforms provide comprehensive analytics dashboards for this purpose. Studying them helps understand how your ads are performing and enable data-driven optimizations.

For a Kickstarter campaign, unlocking the potential of paid advertising on social media is like opening up a vividly vibrant cosmos full of prospective backers. It demands strategic planning, compelling content creation, and constant monitoring. Yet, when done right, it can massively contribute to skyrocketing the success of your campaign.

Chapter 10. Collaboration and Partnerships: Influencer Marketing on Social Media

As we navigate our way through the realm of social media marketing, we encounter an element that has revolutionized today's digital landscape — influencers. Infusing influencer marketing into your Kickstarter campaign can potentially result in significant boosts in visibility, engagement, and ultimately, success. Let us unravel this engaging chapter, comprehensively and meticulously.

10.1. The Influencer Phenomenon

In a time where even one's personal life is but a post away on social media, influencers have emerged as individuals who harness the power of their online presence to sway the preferences, and eventually the actions, of their followers. They come with a ready-made audience, a crowd who trusts them profoundly and highly values their opinions.

Whether it is a tech guru, a parenting blogger, a comic-book maven, or a lifestyle coach, influencers operate in a broad variety of niches, implying that there is an influencer for virtually every Kickstarter campaign that can be conceived. This engaging interplay between influencers' niche-specific content and their followers' interests creates a potent, focused marketing avenue that Kickstarter project owners can utilize.

10.2. Spotting the Right Influencer

Identifying the right influencer is akin to finding the vital key that will unlock a treasure chest of potential backers for your campaign.

It is a task that calls for precision and strategy.

Begin with the basics. Comprehend your campaign's intended reach. Is it local, national, or global? In the world of influencer marketing, size isn't always the most crucial criterion. An influencer with a smaller, but more engaged and localized following could lead to higher conversion rates compared to one with a significant, yet scattered audience.

Next, you want to identify influencers whose content aligns with your campaign. Seek out those who regularly engage with their audience and demonstrate a genuine passion for their field. Look at the influencer's engagement rate, the nature of the comments they receive, and see whether their values resonate with those of your campaign.

10.3. Pitching Your Campaign to Influencers

Once the influencers are identified, the next crucial step is to reach out to them effectively. When crafting your outreach message, remember that it's not just about asking for a favor, but instead, proposing a partnership that could be mutually beneficial.

Your pitch should ideally contain the following:

1. Introduction and brief about your Kickstarter campaign.

2. The reasons why you think the collaboration adds value.

3. Mutually beneficial terms of partnership explicitly spelled out.

Remember, personalization is critical. Each influencer is unique, and their interests vary, thus a one-size-fits-all message might not cut it. Tailor your message to resonate with the particular influencer you're reaching out to, and let them know you appreciate and understand their work.

10.4. The Mechanics of Collaboration

In terms of collaboration, there are several tactics you could employ with influencers. Firstly, product reviews are a win-win situation: The influencer gets unique content while your Kickstarter campaign gets the visibility it needs.

Secondly, giveaways serve as a fantastic technique to attract more engagement and shares. A carefully planned contest (with your campaign's product as the reward, ideally) can spur a wave of traffic and expose your Kickstarter campaign to numerous potential backers.

Moreover, creating an affiliate or referral program provides an opportunity for influencers to earn from the partnership. A personalized referral link or code will motivate influencers to promote your campaign more and will also give you a clear way to track the results of the partnership.

10.5. The Art of Maintaining Influencer Relationships

Influencer partnerships should not be treated as mere transactional relationships. Remember, partnerships are built on mutual respect and shared value; thus, the influencers should be treated as essential collaborators.

It is paramount to keep the conversation ongoing. Even after your campaign concludes, retain these relationships. These influencers can continue to spread the word about your product long after the Kickstarter campaign, aiding you in building a community around your brand.

In summary, influencer marketing provides an exciting opportunity to amplify the reach of your Kickstarter campaign. It enables you to leverage the trust and rapport that influencers have with their followers. Identifying the right influencers, pitching your campaign tactfully, crafting a beneficial collaboration, and maintaining lasting relationships are the keys that will guide you in making the most of this dynamic digital strategy. The road to Kickstarter success awaits, laden with the promise of exciting collaborations and steeped in the thrill of innovative social media strategies.

Chapter 11. Maintaining Momentum: Post-Campaign Strategies and Community Building

Maintaining momentum post-campaign can be just as decisive as the journey towards funding. Post-campaign strategies and community building are integral to harness the trajectory of success established during your campaign period. These actions not only aid in establishing your brand but also pave the way for future projects. Let's delve into this critical area with an exhaustive examination.

11.1. From Pledges to Customers: Fostering Relationships

After a successful campaign, it's vital to remember that you now have not just backers, but customers. They've put their trust in you, and it's crucial to demonstrate that their faith was not misplaced. It's a good time to shift your focus to customer service — addressing concerns, providing updates, and being responsive.

Honest and consistent communication comes into play here. Keeping backers in the loop about key developments, potential challenges, and delivery timelines fosters trust and goodwill. This level of transparency also teaches backers about the process of bringing a project to life, making them feel included and valued.

It's also beneficial to use tools or platforms that allow you to collect customer feedback. This can provide invaluable insight into how your product is being used and perceived, helping you to make improvements for future iterations and even sparking ideas for new products or services to develop.

11.2. The Power of Continued Presence

In the era of social media, out of sight can mean out of mind. Hence, continuing your online presence is essential. You should consistently provide updates about your project or product even after your campaign ends. This continued conversation can involve behind-the-scenes peeks, production updates, or highlighting user-generated content. The key is to keep backers feeling connected to your journey.

Do not fail to leverage the sense of community established during the campaign. Harness the community feeling by inviting backers to share their own experiences or ideas. This can take the form of social media posts, online forums, or regular newsletters.

11.3. Spotlight on Community Engagement

Your Kickstarter success has brought together a community bonded by a shared interest in your project. This community's continued engagement bears the potential for immense mutual gains.

Community-focused strategies like creating an online discussion forum or initiating engagement activities can keep the momentum going. This could include AMA (Ask Me Anything) sessions, fan art contests, or thematic discussion boards. Remember, what you aim for is a thriving, active community that extends beyond transactional interactions and dives deep into experiential resonances.

Invite constructive conversations by asking open-ended questions and taking a keen interest in the responses. Validate the community's contributions regularly and ensure that their efforts are recognized.

11.4. Pursuit of Future Projects: Building Upon Success

With the community supporting you and the first successful Kickstarter project under your belt, the time may be ripe to think about future initiatives. Launching new projects not only keeps the momentum going but also gives existing backers a fresh reason to invest in you again.

This, however, comes with the responsibility of learning from your previous experience. Reflect on what worked well and what didn't during your first campaign. Carry forward the positive aspects and work on the areas that need improvement.

Regardless of your future outcomes, remember that the community you've built is your golden asset. It is essential to nurture this community before, during, and after every campaign you launch.

In conclusion, maintaining momentum post-campaign is a nuanced process requiring constant vigilance and active customer engagement. While the campaign's end may seem like the journey's end, it often signals the beginning of an even more enriching phase. The strategies and community outlined here are more than just post-campaign elements - they are the building blocks for establishing a lasting brand and enjoying sustained success.